Stocks

Guide and Tips from Beginner to Pro with different Marketing Style to boost your Stocks and Earn More!

By James Stevens

Published by Shepal Publishing

Table of Contents

Introduction

The financial market provides people with an opportunity to grow their money. This can be done in several ways, including the short term where it is possible to make a return on a daily basis, or the long term, where investment takes several years and provide a bountiful return. Buying and selling stocks is one way through which one can benefit from investing in the financial markets. Stocks gives an investor a chance to own part of a business instead of establishing their own business, and this comes with so many benefits and great returns on their investments in the long run.

There are so many things that are involved in the buying of stocks that you need to know about if you are new to the financial market. You need to know the different kinds of stocks that you can invest or trade in. New investors should clearly understand how to buy their stocks and the criteria of choosing the right stocks to invest in. You also require to know some trading styles to chose from if you decide to start trading in stocks. This information is available in this eBook, together with stock investing tips that will help you along the way and reveal to you how you can maximize your returns and minimize your losses once you start trading or investing in stocks.

Start by mastering a few financial terms, then take off on the right note. This is just what every beginner needs to get started.

Chapter 1:
Stocks Basics

A stock is a type of security that gives the buyer part ownership of a business as well as a right to claim ownership of the business's assets and its earnings. The buyer becomes the shareholder and this means that he is an owner of the business. Ownership is determined by the number of stocks one has. There are basically two types of stocks:

- Common stocks

- Preferred stocks

The common stocks are those that give the buyer the right to vote in a shareholder's meeting as well as to receive dividends when the business makes some profit.

The preferred stocks on the other hand do not carry any voting rights for the buyer but the buyer has a higher claim on the business's assets and on the business' earnings compared to the common shareholder. A shareholder of preferred stock will receive dividends before a common shareholder and they are always the first to be compensated in case the business gets liquidated.

Stocks are also called shares, equities or securities because by buying them, you get an equity or part ownership of the business or you are securing a share of the business.

Basic terms used in stock investing

There are many terms that are used in stock investing that a beginner investor need to be aware of. They are important to learn so that you will have an easy time communicating to other investors and people in the financial markets. Some of these are:

a) Portfolio: This is a collection of investments that are owned by a single investor.

b) Broker: This is the person who will buy and sell stocks for you for a commission.

c) Dividend: This is the amount of money an investor gets after a company makes a profit.

d) Quotes: This is the information pertaining to a stock's latest trading price.

e) Averaging down: This is buying more of a stock as the prices go down.

f) Order: This is your bid to buy or sell stocks of a certain amount of money

g) Execution: This means that an order that you placed to buy or sell shares has been completed.

h) Bear market: The period of time when the prices of stocks go down

i) Bull market: The opposite of the bear market, and it means a long time period of an increase in stock prices.

j) Day trading: A trading strategy where you buy and sell stocks on the same day before the market closes.

k) Margin: This is a type of account which allows investors to borrow some money from their broker to make an investment.

l) Blue Chip Stocks: These are the large and leading companies in different industries.

m) Yield: The value of the return of an investment you made. It is mainly measured by the amount of dividend you get annually or quarterly.

n) Volatility: The changes in stock price.

o) Spread: The difference between the bid and the ask price in reference to a certain stock. It is the difference between the amount a seller is willing to sell a certain shock and the amount a buyer is willing to pay for it.

How stocks trade

Most stocks trade on exchanges, where buyers and sellers meet and agree on the stock price. There are both physical trading floors and there are online stock exchanges. The stock market facilitates stock trading and ensures that both the buyers and the sellers are benefitting from their investments. The market reduces the risk of investing as well, for the benefit of both the buyers and the sellers.

The prices of stocks change every day due to various forces in the stock market. The prices of one stock can go up or down due to demand and supply. The changes in the price of a business's stock is the one that determines its worth, and this is what determines if people will like its stocks or not. Even though the value of a business is largely determined by its market capitalization, its stock price matters since it also determines the future performance of the company, and this is what tells investors what they can expect from their investments in the future.

Other than the stock price, the earnings of a company should matter to an investor. This is the amount of profits a business is making, and this information is normally available in the financial reports and journals.

The main reason why stock prices fluctuate every day is so varied it would be a challenge trying to pinpoint what has occurred. It depends on what is happening within the company, and also the external economic environment. What investors need to know is that stocks are volatile and their prices can change rapidly, therefore it is not always easy to know when to buy and when to sell stocks in order not to lose in the end. A lot of trading strategies have come up though, which helps investors in determining how much risk they are willing to take in the process of trading a stock.

Chapter 2:
Choosing Stocks to Invest In

There is a lot of information online pertaining to various companies which can guide you to the right stocks to invest in. You have to take time to perform an analysis in order to select the right stocks to invest in. The last thing you need is to make a mistake in the choice of stock because you will end up losing your money and time. If you have an idea of the type of companies that you want to invest in, go through their websites to find information relating to their stocks. Look for their financial reports as well in order to determine if the company is doing well in the market or not as this is the most important consideration. It is best to understand all the financial information you get about a company before you make the final investment decision.

It is important to choose to invest in a business that is doing well. This will give you peace of mind that your investment will not go to waste and that you will be able to enjoy a worthwhile return. There are a few indications you should look out for in order to determine whether the company is doing well or not. These include: -

- The company's profit margin

- A company's return on equity

- Past performance and expected growth

- Its historic rate of earnings growth compared to its peers

- The debts that the company has

- The debt-to-equity ratio which basically means taking the company's debt and dividing it by shareholder equity. The lower the percentage is, the better and safer your investment will be.

Here are some factors that will help you make the right choice of stock to invest in:

1. Effective business management- This is in fact the most important factor to consider when one is choosing stocks to invest in. However, not many investors are able to access how effective the business management is, therefore they do not consider this. Return on equity and the income shareholders earn per their investments is a great indication of how the business management uses the money investors have invested into the business. A business with a return on equity of 5% or more is a good one to consider investing in.

2. Stocks from a suitable business sector- It is important to choose the industry sectors where you want to invest in wisely. Some sectors do better than the others, which is why this is important. You do not have to invest all your money in just one sector; this can in fact be risky for your investment. When you are diversifying, only go for stocks in the leading industry sectors to ensure that at least all your stocks will be performing well. If after sometime you will want to invest more money, you will invest in the sector that is doing better than the others. If there is a sector that is not doing well and you have already invested in it, you can always withdraw your investment as soon as possible, then reinvest the money in a better performing sector.

3. The growing profits- It is very important to invest in a company that is already making profits. A company that has growing profits is even better. Go for a company whose earnings per share growth is steady and at least 5% or more. This is what will assure you that you will be getting some money at the end of every year for as long as you will be investing in that company.

4. The size of the company- Small companies are more risky to invest in when compared to the big companies. The big companies that have already established themselves already know how to survive in the market therefore it is hard for such companies to go down. That is why they are the best to invest in. If possible, avoid penny stocks unless if you are willing to deal with all the risks involved. However, if you want to invest in stocks that can guarantee you something every year, it is good to consider investing in the big businesses.

5. Manageable debt- A business can borrow money in order to build itself but too much debt is not good for the business. It is important to check this out before you decide to invest your money so that you will know if the debt per capital ratio is healthy or not. A rate of 0.5 or less is a good one but if it is more then there will be a problem thereafter. A business that is in debts will not be able to compensate its investors and you might end up losing all your investment in the repayment of those debts.

6. Dividend payments- Companies that return part of their profits to the investors in terms of dividends are good companies to invest in. A dividend payment of 2% or more is a good one to consider, therefore this is an important factor too. Dividends are additional financial

benefits that every investor should consider when investing their money. This is where the return on your investment on an annual basis comes in.

7. Stocks with sufficient liquidity- These are stocks that can easily be sold out if you no longer want to continue owning them. Some stocks are hard to sell and these will give you a lot of problems when you finally want to sell them off. It is good to consider investing in stocks that will allow you to sell your position as fast as you want when the need arises.

Chapter 3:
Buying Your First Stocks

This is normally the most challenging step for many beginner investors, as it is the first time that they take a risk, hoping it will eventually pay off. Many master the basics but they do not get to the buying bit because they do not know how to go about it. It is quite simple. There are three main ways through which one can buy stocks:

1. Using a broker

This is the most common ways to purchase stocks. Brokers help when it comes to chasing stocks and even selling stocks for investors. First time stock investors can benefit from the support of brokers before you learn how the market operates to be able to manage your own account. There are two types of brokers you can choose from:

The full-service broker: This one will offer you his full time services as well as professional advice on stock investing. He will be the one responsible for managing your account. This kind of broker charges a little more than other brokers. A few years ago, these were the only stock brokers available and so, only a few people could afford their services. These days, people are able to manage their accounts and they can now afford the other types of broker with ease.

Discount brokers: These ones do not have as many terms and conditions as the full-service broker, which is what makes them considerably cheaper. The internet is helping a lot of investors start independent trade, though if you have no idea what you should do to begin with, you can use the services of this type of broker to maximize your returns while gaining professional advice.

2. Through dividends reinvestment plans

This is a plan whereby individual companies allow investors to purchase more stocks following an initial investment, through reinvesting the dividends that they get annually or quarterly. This is a great way to invest as it allows an investor to start off with an investment which is a small amount of money. When one has a long term aim, this is an ideal way to grow that small investment with minimal risk.

3. Direct Investment Plans

These are plans by individual companies to allow investors to buy stocks directly from the company for a small fee.

Picking a stock to invest in

If you have already made up your mind to start investing, it is time to pick the stocks to invest in. It is recommended that you have a portfolio, which is a selection of different stocks in different sectors. Always diversify your portfolio across many sectors as this helps to spread your risk as opposed to investing all your money in just one business. There are many stocks to choose from and one can easily get confused about the right ones to invest in. Many people rely on financial information about the companies they are interested in, which is a good though not fully reliable. There are other important factors that will help you make the right choice and these include:

i) Your goals: This is the purpose you have for your portfolio and it is the main consideration you should have in mind whenever you are picking out stocks to trade. Investors have their investing goals based on capital preservation, capital appreciation and the expected income and this is what influences the choices that are made. Investors focusing on capital preservation for instance will always go for low risk businesses in order to minimize their losses. Income-oriented investors on the other hand will go for low-growing firms which guarantee something at the end of the month.

ii) Stay up to date with current market events and opinions: Investors have to always keep an open eye on the happenings of the stock market. This will help you in deciding which stocks you will invest in. Ensure that you have all the information about the stocks you are considering, how they perform, and the benefits the people who have already invested in the stocks are enjoying as well as their opinions pertaining to the future of those stocks. For this kind of information, blogs, financial magazines and financial online news should be part of your daily life. The internet has made access to information very easy and new investors need to capitalize on this for the best decision making.

iii) Find companies that could be good to invest in: With thousands of companies in numerous, knowing what to choose and where will not be a simple task. However, with a little help, you can come up with a list of potential companies that could interest you with ease. A financial adviser can help you narrow down your options to a few of the best companies that you can invest in. Information in blogs and financial statements can help in this as well. ETF holdings will enable a quicker search of the best performers in every industry. Compare each of them in detail to arrive at the best for your investment.

Reading a stock quote

Every financial table has financial stocks that investors should be able to read and understand. The advantage of investing in this modern era is that you can easily access stock quotes from different companies online. This is an advantage because many companies update their quotes everyday and these quotes come with comprehensive information that can help you understand the information provided better. There are major financial websites that you can use to get financial information of any kind, for instance Yahoo!, Finance, among others.

Chapter 4:
Investing in Dividends, Foreign and Penny Stocks

The challenge many new investors face is in deciding the right place to invest their money is where they will get the most gain. Even with the right kind of information, one is always skeptical about the success of an investment that they are about to take. New investors should know that investing involves risk taking; things can work in your favor or against your favor, therefore there is need for preparedness of any outcome.

Investing in Dividend Stocks

If you are looking for a long term investment strategy, you will benefit from a wide choice of high quality dividend paying stocks. The result of this investment is an extended period of great returns and a chance to enjoy a dependable dividend income.

Choosing dividend paying stocks

Not all stocks earn dividends, therefore if you are specifically looking for those that will earn you some dividends annually or quarterly, you have to choose wisely.

You need to learn how stocks yield dividends first, then you can pick out potential stocks to choose from. This will require you to screen several companies, looking to ascertain their profitability, how much is retained, and how much is paid out as dividends to shareholders. This information is often available on a financial statement. Go for dividend achievers;

these are those stocks that show consistent increase in their dividend payout amounts.

Choosing a high quality stock

Once you have a list of dividend paying stocks, you want to ensure that you are dealing with only high quality stocks. To make the right choice, look out for the following:

- Uninterrupted dividend payment- check financial information of the company dating back as far as ten years

- Look out for high return on equity. Check for a five-year average of about 15-20%

- Look out for rising sales and rising earnings per share.

- Look for dividend growth. The best company will be the one with growth of about 5% or more over the last ten years.

With such information, you can rank the companies in your list and choose to invest your money on the company that comes out as the best.

Investing in foreign stocks

Foreign stocks attract many experienced investors, though even a beginner can also trade in them. Foreign companies are quite promising and an investor can enjoy high returns but there is elevated risk that should not be ignored. The other challenge you could face if you want to invest in foreign stocks is choosing the right company to invest in. This requires detailed research of the other country, the different sectors as well as the economy.

The advantages of investing in foreign stocks include: -

- Foreign stocks represent an added investment opportunity. You may not get the right company to invest in locally but you can get one internationally depending on what you are looking for.

- It is a way to diversify. You need to spread the risk of your investment by investing in more than one company, and this could represent itself in terms of foreign stocks.

The risks of investing in foreign stocks should not be overlooked. There are pretty serious risks that investors should be aware of, for instance the exchange rate risk. Your return on a stock could end up catering for currency exchange rates from the foreign country's currency to your country's currency. The economy of the country will determine how much you gain or lose from fluctuating exchange rates. Those countries that suffer from political and social issues are quite risky to invest in.

However, all these risks bring great rewards in the end. As financial experts would say, the higher the risk, the greater the returns. If you are able to pick out a company to invest in, you can expect big rewards if things turn out according to your plan.

Investing in Penny Stocks

Penny stocks are those kinds of stocks with small share prices, which allows many people access to the financial markets, even when they do not have a large amount of money to invest. Investors with just a small amount of money can own a good number of penny stocks. This comes with benefits and disadvantages to the investor. The main advantage is that they are affordable. Unlike the highly valuable stocks, which you have to invest a huge sum of money to afford a few stocks, you can easily own a good number of penny stocks with a much smaller investment.

However, any negative movement in the value of the stock, no matter how minor it could be, can have a large impact on penny stocks and your expected overall return. Many trades associated with penny stocks are usually unregulated, which is a risk that you should be aware of.

If you want to invest in penny stocks, follow these guidelines:

1. Always read the warnings provided by regulators

2. Do your own background check

3. Be aware of the company's level of disclosure

4. Be sure that this is what you really want

Chapter 5:
Stock Trading Styles

Stock trading basically entails frequent buying and selling of stocks in order to make more returns than an investor who buys and holds for future benefits. Traders make profits, which are the incomes they receive from their investments and this is enjoyed on a regular basis. Traders aim at buying low and selling high and the difference in stock price is what they capitalize in so as to make some profits by the end of the trading period. The trading period is usually short, and this is mainly determined by a trader's style. There are four main trading styles one can choose from when trading in stocks:

1. **Position trading**: This is the longest trading period. Trades here can take months to years, and this enables them to take more time to evaluate the trends in the market before they can make a decision to either buy or sell. Position trading is skewed more towards investing but traders here are open to long term and short term trading strategies, unlike investors who only focus on long term trades. Position traders therefore use weekly and monthly charts in order to make the right decision when trading. They will ignore the short term price changes and focus on the long term changes in order to make a solid decision and enjoy more returns from their investments.

2. **Day trading**: This is a trading style in which a trading position is entered and exited on the same day. A day trader will not be allowed to hold any positions overnight; he should be done as soon as the market closes. This means that a trader can stop at a loss or even at a profit if his target has been achieved. Day

traders benefit a lot from technical analysis in order to utilize intraday price changes in the stocks they are trading in. They will watch an intraday price chart the entire day just to look out for a trading opportunity.

Day traders do not get to enjoy huge profits because their trading positions are held for hours to minutes and significant price changes do not happen in a day. What they capitalize on are the small and frequent profits that they are likely to make if they make the right decisions after a change in price of a stock they are trading in. Most day traders trade for a living because they have to monitor the stock price movements the entire day.

3. **Swing trading**: This is a stock trading style where trading positions are held for days to weeks. Traders here focus on short term price fluctuations in order to make a profitable trade. Technical analysis helps swing traders as well as any change on the stock price as this is what they capitalize on so as to sell or buy the stocks they are interested in. The fundamentals of a company do not matter so much to a swing trader because a trader will exit when he has attained his trading goals for the day. Traders using this trading style do not have to monitor the stock price changes in detail because the trading position is held for just a few days. This is therefore the trading style for traders who have less time to monitor the stock market closely.

4. **Scalp trading**: This is related to day trading; it is a more active form of day trading that involves a frequent buying and selling of stocks throughout the trading session. The day to day changes in stock prices are the making focus of scalp traders. They are comfortable

with the small but frequent profits that they make through frequent buying and selling of stocks.

Trading positions here are held for seconds to minutes and scalp traders have to be keen every minute in order to take advantage of any change in price of stocks they are trading in for a gain. In order to maximize their returns, scalp traders may place many trades at the same time, which is highly risky and also highly profitable in case things work in their favor. A scalp trader is a full time trader because he has to monitor the stock market closely at all times.

Choosing a trading style is not easy but it does not have to be hard at all if you know what you are looking for in the stock market. There are a number of factors one needs to take into consideration when choosing a trading style to go for:

1. Your account size

2. The amount of time you have for trading

3. Your trading experience level

4. Your risk tolerance

5. Your personality

Basically speaking, the amount of time one has for trading will determine by a large percentage the kind of trading style you will go for. A person who has only a few hours in a week to monitor financial and stock charts for instance will be a better position trader, but one who has all the time in the day to closely monitor the stock market will be a better day trader or scalp trader. Traders can also trade in more than one trading style.

Chapter 6:
Stock Investment Rules
Investors Must Follow

Many investors are lured into stock investments because they want to make a large amount of money in a short period of time. Once they make the investment they realize that things are not as easy as they previously thought and frustrations start creeping in. Stock investing requires a lot of information, patience and discipline. You also need to conduct in-depth research into the market in order to understand how the market operates. This is the only way you will know the rules of stock investing and how you can increase your chances of making more money. What investors need to know is that there is no sure way to make so much money in the stock markets. You have much to gain from a few stock investing rules, which if followed well can increase your chances of reaping big with your investment. These include:-

1. Avoid the crowd mentality- Many people make their final buying decision after the influence of their acquaintances, friends, neighbors, realities and other important people in their lives. This is a huge mistake because you are unable to think clearly about what is best for you and what is not. If everyone around you was investing in a certain stock, all other investors will be doing the same and this ends up backfiring on everyone. You need to avoid as much as possible following other people's decisions. Just like a great investor once said, be afraid when all others are greedy and be greedy when all others are being afraid. This is what will give you something to enjoy out of your investment.

2. Always follow a disciplined investment approach- The reason many people fail in stock investing is because they are indisciplined. Like mentioned earlier, one thing that will lead to a successful investment is discipline. Aim at putting your money systematically in the right shares and hold onto your investments patiently until you see an opportunity to make some profits. You should not be in a rush to make some money even when you cannot clearly see an opportunity to trade, nor should you be in a hurry to recover what you have lost in the previous trade. Patience is what will help you maintain a disciplined approach to stock trading. Also, always keep a long term general picture in mind, which is what you want to achieve after sometime not in the short term and this will help you trade wisely.

3. Do not time the market- Trying to time the stock market is the reason why a lot of stock investors are losing so much money every day. It is impossible to catch the tops and the bottoms and to effectively sell or by a position. Stick to your trading rules, trading strategies and your trading time and you will avoid making a costly mistake. Financial planners always insist that trying to time the stock market backfires on investors and they are right, because this is what happens every time an investor tries to outsmart the stock market. Things change in a span of seconds, which is why many investors end up losing.

4. Only invest in your surplus funds- One thing that stock investors need to learn and stick to is investing the money which they can afford to lose. Gaining and losing is the order of the game in the stock markets, therefore do not invest all the money you have hoping to gain,

because this can kill your financial position if things do not turn out well. The stock market is very unstable, that is why you only need to deal with surplus funds which you can afford to lose. This does not mean that you should always be prepared to lose; there is a chance that your investment will gain you huge profits in the long run. With that in mind, you should invest then work hard to ensure that you are not losing that money. This is through making the right choices at all times and waiting patiently even for a small chance to make some profits.

5. Do not allow emotions to cloud your judgment- Your ability to control your emotions will help you so much in keeping your investment safe. People get emotional and then they make irrational decisions which end up costing them all or a large part of their investment. Fear and greed are the major emotions that are associated with stock investing. Sometimes you are faced with a possibility of making so much money and that urge to get rich quickly is hard to resist. What investors do not know is that where there is a high chance to make so much money, there is also an equal chance of losing so much money, therefore you can either gain a lot or lose so much.

Greed is what makes investors speculate and buy shares of unknown companies or even to create big positions without thinking twice about the risks that are involved in all that especially in the bull market. When the market reverses, you will end up losing so much money instead of creating the wealth you had anticipated. In a bear market on the other hand, fear drives investors to sell their shares at a very low price and they end up losing all the money that they have invested in the

25

stocks. If you want to service in the stock market, you have to gain total control over your emotions particularly these two emotions.

6. Maintain realistic expectations- It is always good to hope for the best in anything that you do but when it comes to stock investing, you should be careful about what you hope to achieve as this is what drives one to make irrational decisions just to ensure that their expectations are met in the end. It is continuously good to think of all the possible outcomes and ensure that you can embrace them equally so as to avoid stress and emotional trading in case you get what you did not expect. Sometimes you will gain so much money out of your investment but this does not mean that things will always be like this; there are those days when you will lose, and life should go on. Do not allow your unrealistic assumptions to drive you crazy because this will lead you to trouble.

Chapter 7:
Stock Investing Tips that Work

Information will always help you significantly when you are investing, as you will be able to make investment decisions based on fact rather than hunches. There is just so much that new investors need to know before they can invest their money in stocks. With the right information, investment tips will help you in doing the right thing at the right time. Many people who make the wrong investment decisions are those that fail in just a little thing. These investment tips will help you avoid the little mistakes that could cost you a lot of money in the long run.

1. Always have your expectations in place.

Many people think of the financial market as a place where they can easily double their investment in no time at all, that is why many stock investors go into stock trades expecting to make huge returns. This will frustrate you if that has been your mindset. One thing that will work out well for you is to maintain the right expectations. This will help you stay calm and help you to accept any outcome. Unreasonable expectations will often result in irrational decisions that could be highly risky and before you know it, you have lost so much money in a short period of time. This will have a great impact on your capital and you may find it a challenge to get back on your feet.

2. Behave like the business owner

Investing in stocks gives you certain rights over the business, therefore you have to start thinking like the owner even before you invest in the business. This way, you will be able to act with conviction and not impulsively. As the owner of the business, you will need to understand in detail how the business operates, to go through its financial reports so that you can tell how it is performing and also to think of what its future will be like. This will help you in coming up with a list of the best investable companies that you can consider to include in your investment portfolio.

3. Focus

There are so many distractions out there that can easily influence your decision making. What you need to do is to turn a deaf ear to all of them and focus on what is important to you. The media nowadays is taking part in capturing the investor's attention for the benefit of individual companies. What they say is what they want you to hear, and this will not help your decision making in any way.

You have to focus on what you want and conduct your own research so that you will understand the companies better. If you were to pay attention to the media alone, you will never understand the actual reason why the prices of stocks change in most of the companies. You are better off working on your own and digging out information on your own. After all you are the only one who understands what you are looking for in every investment that you make.

4. Buy low and sell high

This is the only way you will get something big out of your investment. Do not wait to buy when the stocks have risen because this is the time their prices are high. Many people who do this end up selling when the prices are down. Look out for when the stocks have fallen and this is the right time to buy because the prices are usually low at that particular period of time. When the stocks skyrocket, they are high and this is the right time to sell because the prices are usually high.

5. Watch out for the trend

The past trend of a business is a good indication of the direction that the business will take in the future, which will be a key influence when you are investing. In as much as this is not the only indication of the value of a business, the past trend will help you to properly shape your expectations. Therefore, when you are investing, you should be on the lookout for those companies that have been performing pretty well in the past, particularly during hard economic times.

Conclusion

The popularity of stock market is increasing everyday as it is currently amongst the best places to invest your money in. So many people have realized this and they are now enjoying profits and building their investment portfolios for future gains. Even though investing in stocks is risky, managing the risks is very easy too, but only if you have the right tools at hand. One thing that you should take advantage of in order to shine in the stock market is information. Many investors do not take time to understand the financial markets better that is why they fail terribly. You have to be smart and arm yourself with deeply insightful research in order to make smart moves at all times for the profits.

Smart investing in the stock market does not only give you the great feeling of being a pro investor but a lot of other financial benefits that are worth your attention. You can get to enjoy numerous investment gains, which include a chance for you to grow your money over a period of time. The amount of money you invest in stocks is not what you get in the end; you get a lot more. Another major benefit you should look out for is a chance to enjoy regular income from your investment. This makes stock market worthy of anyone's attention.

This guide has been designed to help you get started well in stock investing and stock trading so that you can enjoy all these and many more benefits from your investments.

www.ingramcontent.com/pod-product-compliance
Lightning Source LLC
Chambersburg PA
CBHW070430190526
45169CB00003B/1491